APPEARANCE 3

HABITAT AND DISTRIBUTION 3

BEHAVIOR AND COMPATIBILITY 3

EARLY HISTORY AND DISCOVERY 6

PHYSICAL CHARACTERISTICS AND ANATOMY 8

GENETICS AND COLOR VARIETIES 11

HYBRID: CROSSBREEDING AND ITS CONSEQUENCES 14

QUARANTINE PROCEDURES FOR NEW FISH 17

NATIVE HABITAT AND DISTRIBUTION 20

BEHAVIOR AND SOCIAL STRUCTURE 23

FEEDING HABITS AND DIET 26

REPRODUCTION AND BREEDING CYCLE 29

WATER PARAMETERS AND TEMPERATURE REQUIREMENTS 32

TANKMATES: COMPATIBLE SPECIES 35

TERRITORIALITY AND HIERARCHY 38

REPRODUCTION AND BREEDING CYCLE 41

COMMON DISEASES AND HEALTH ISSUES 44

RECOGNIZING AND TREATING COMMON DISEASES 47

PREVENTION AND TREATMENT OF DISEASES 50

LIFE CYCLE AND GROWTH STAGES 53

SELECTING HEALTHY FISH: BUYING AND QUARANTINE PROCESS ... 55

HYBRIDIZATION: CROSSBREEDING AND ITS CONSEQUENCES 58

PREPARING FOR BREEDING 61

SPAWNING PROCESS AND PARENTAL CARE 64

RAISING FISH FRY: CARE AND FEEDING 66

TANK TROUBLESHOOTING: ALGAE CONTROL AND WATER QUALITY ISSUES 69

AQUATIC PLANTS: SUITABLE CHOICES 72

CARING FOR FRY: RAISING THE NEXT GENERATION 75

AQUASCAPING FOR TANKS 78

CREATING COMMUNITY TANKS 81

IN THE WILD: OBSERVATIONS AND STUDIES 84

CONCLUSION 87

Moonlight Gourami

The Moonlight Gourami, scientifically known as Trichopodus microlepis, is a freshwater fish species belonging to the gourami family. It is popular among aquarium enthusiasts for its stunning appearance and peaceful nature.

Appearance

The Moonlight Gourami showcases a graceful body with a distinct laterally compressed shape. It can grow up to 4-6 inches (10-15 cm) in length. The fish has a silvery-white to pale blue body coloration, which gives it a shimmering and ethereal appearance, resembling moonlight. The fins are long and flowing, adding to its beauty.

Habitat and Distribution

Moonlight Gouramis are native to Southeast Asia, specifically found in Thailand, Malaysia, and Indonesia. They inhabit slow-moving rivers, streams, and flooded areas with dense vegetation. In the wild, they prefer areas with plenty of hiding spots, such as submerged tree roots and aquatic plants.

Behavior and Compatibility

These gouramis are generally peaceful and can be kept in community aquariums with other peaceful fish species. However, caution should be exercised when housing them with aggressive or fin-nipping fish, as the Moonlight Gourami's flowing fins can be a target for aggression.

Diet

Moonlight Gouramis are omnivorous and will readily accept a varied diet. In their natural habitat, they feed on insects, small crustaceans, algae, and plant matter. In aquariums, they can be fed a combination of high-quality flakes, pellets, frozen or live foods such as brine shrimp, bloodworms, and daphnia. Offering a balanced diet ensures their overall health and vibrant coloration.

Care and Tank Requirements

When it comes to keeping Moonlight Gouramis, a spacious aquarium with plenty of hiding places is essential. Provide ample vegetation, driftwood, and rocks to create a natural environment. Maintain a stable water temperature between 75-82°F (24-28°C) and keep the pH slightly acidic to neutral, around 6.5-7.5. They are tolerant of a wide range of water conditions, but sudden fluctuations should be avoided.

Breeding

Moonlight Gouramis are bubble nest builders, and breeding them can be a rewarding experience. To encourage breeding, provide floating plants or a styrofoam cup as a nest-building site. The male will construct a nest and entice the female to spawn beneath it. Once the eggs are laid, the male will guard the nest until the fry hatch. The fry can be fed infusoria and later transitioned to baby brine shrimp or crushed flakes.

In conclusion, the Moonlight Gourami is a captivating fish species known for its beautiful appearance and peaceful demeanor. With proper care and suitable tank conditions, they can thrive and add a touch of elegance to any freshwater aquarium.

Moonlight Gourami

Early History and Discovery

The early history and discovery of the Moonlight Gourami are intertwined with the exploration of Southeast Asia and the study of its diverse aquatic life.

Exploration of Southeast Asia

In the 19th century, various explorers and naturalists embarked on expeditions to the Southeast Asian region, including Thailand, Malaysia, and Indonesia. These expeditions aimed to document the rich biodiversity found in the area, both on land and in water.

Discovery of the Moonlight Gourami

The Moonlight Gourami was first discovered and described by European naturalists during these exploratory ventures. While the exact details of its initial discovery are unclear, it is believed to have been documented and classified as a species in the late 1800s or early 1900s.

The scientific name of the Moonlight Gourami, Trichopodus microlepis, was assigned by the taxonomist George Albert Boulenger in 1897. Boulenger was a renowned Belgian-British ichthyologist who made significant contributions to the study of fish taxonomy during his time.

Importance in the Aquarium Trade

Following its discovery, the Moonlight Gourami gained popularity in the aquarium trade due to its captivating appearance. The fish's shimmering silvery-white to pale blue coloration and graceful fins made it a sought-after species among aquarium enthusiasts.

Over the years, selective breeding efforts have led to the development of various color morphs and strains of Moonlight Gouramis, further enhancing their desirability in the aquarium hobby.

Today, the Moonlight Gourami continues to be appreciated by aquarists worldwide, showcasing the beauty of Southeast Asian aquatic fauna and serving as a reminder of the importance of conservation efforts in preserving these species for future generations.

Moonlight Gourami

Physical Characteristics and Anatomy

The Moonlight Gourami possesses distinct physical characteristics and anatomy that contribute to its allure and adaptation to its environment.

Body Shape and Size

The Moonlight Gourami has a graceful and laterally compressed body shape. It typically grows to a length of 4-6 inches (10-15 cm) when fully mature. The elongated body allows for efficient movement through the water and contributes to its elegant appearance.

Coloration

The primary attraction of the Moonlight Gourami lies in its mesmerizing coloration. The fish exhibits a silvery-white to pale blue hue, which resembles the soft glow of moonlight. This unique coloration gives the species its name and distinguishes it from other gourami species.

Fins

The Moonlight Gourami possesses long and flowing fins, which add to its beauty and elegance. The dorsal fin, located on the back of the fish, is elongated and often extends towards the caudal fin. The caudal fin itself is fan-shaped and aids in propulsion and maneuverability.

Labyrinth Organ

Like other gouramis, the Moonlight Gourami possesses a specialized organ known as the labyrinth organ. This organ allows the fish to breathe atmospheric air by gulping it from the water's surface. The labyrinth organ is an adaptation to the oxygen-poor environments, such as stagnant or oxygen-depleted waters, where the species can be found in the wild.

Scales and Adaptations

The Moonlight Gourami's body is covered in small, cycloid scales that provide protection and minimize friction in the water. These scales are iridescent, enhancing the fish's shimmering appearance. The gourami's scales also aid in thermoregulation, helping it adapt to a wide range of water temperatures.

Sensory Organs

The Moonlight Gourami possesses a range of sensory organs to navigate its environment and locate prey. It has well-developed eyes that enable it to see in various lighting conditions. The fish also has a pair of long, sensitive barbels, called maxillary barbels, located near its mouth. These barbels aid in locating food and detecting changes in water currents.

In conclusion, the Moonlight Gourami showcases a unique combination of physical characteristics and anatomical features, including its graceful body shape, captivating coloration, flowing fins, labyrinth organ, protective scales, and sensory adaptations. These attributes contribute to its beauty, adaptability, and overall appeal in both natural habitats and aquarium settings.

Moonlight Gourami

Genetics and Color Varieties

The Moonlight Gourami, Trichopodus microlepis, exhibits fascinating genetics and various color varieties that have been selectively bred to enhance its visual appeal.

Genetics of Coloration

The unique coloration of the Moonlight Gourami is influenced by genetic factors. The specific genes responsible for its silvery-white to pale blue coloration have not been extensively studied, but it is believed to involve a combination of pigments, structural proteins, and iridescence.

Genetic variations within Moonlight Gourami populations contribute to slight differences in color intensity, brightness, and pattern. Selective breeding practices have focused on maintaining and enhancing the desirable color traits to produce visually striking specimens.

Color Varieties

Through selective breeding, several color varieties of the Moonlight Gourami have been developed. These color morphs showcase different shades and patterns while retaining the characteristic silvery-white to pale blue base color.

Opaline Moonlight Gourami

The Opaline Moonlight Gourami is a popular variant that displays an opalescent sheen over its base color. This opalescence is caused by structural characteristics of the scales, which reflect and scatter light, creating a stunning visual effect.

Gold Moonlight Gourami

The Gold Moonlight Gourami is another sought-after variety. It exhibits a golden hue, ranging from a pale yellow to a rich, deep gold coloration. The gold color is achieved through selective breeding and the expression of specific pigments.

Other Variations

In addition to the Opaline and Gold varieties, there may be other color morphs or strains of Moonlight Gouramis available in the aquarium trade. These variations could include subtle differences in color intensity, shimmer, or fin patterning.

It's worth noting that the availability of specific color varieties may vary depending on the region and the breeding efforts of aquarium enthusiasts and fish farms.

Maintenance of Color Varieties

To maintain the vibrant coloration of Moonlight Gouramis, proper care and nutrition are crucial. A well-balanced diet consisting of high-quality flakes, pellets, and occasional live or frozen foods will provide the necessary nutrients for optimal color development. Providing a stress-free and well-maintained aquarium environment with stable water conditions further supports the fish's overall health and color vibrancy.

In conclusion, the Moonlight Gourami exhibits fascinating genetics and offers various color varieties through selective breeding. These color morphs, such as the Opaline and Gold variations, contribute to the visual appeal of this already *captivating species, making it a prized addition to aquariums worldwide.*

Moonlight Gourami

Hybrid: Crossbreeding and Its Consequences

The hybridization of Moonlight Gouramis through crossbreeding has become a subject of interest among aquarium enthusiasts. While hybridization can result in unique and visually striking fish, there are potential consequences that need to be considered.

Crossbreeding in Aquaria

Crossbreeding involves mating individuals of different species or different varieties within the same species. In the case of Moonlight Gouramis, crossbreeding can occur between different gourami species or between different color varieties of the same species.

Consequences of Hybridization

When hybridization occurs, there are several potential consequences that need to be taken into account:

Genetic Integrity

Hybridization can result in a loss of genetic integrity within the purebred populations. As hybrid offspring are produced, the unique genetic traits of the parent species or varieties may be diluted or altered, potentially leading to the loss of desirable characteristics or genetic diversity.

Fertility and Viability

Hybrids may exhibit reduced fertility or viability compared to the parent species. This reduced fertility can limit the successful reproduction of hybrids, potentially resulting in a smaller population and decreased availability of purebred specimens.

Health and Adaptability

Hybrids may also face challenges in terms of health and adaptability. The combination of genetic traits from different species or varieties may result in individuals that are less well-suited to their natural environment or more prone to certain health issues. This can affect their overall well-being and longevity.

Ethical Considerations

There are ethical considerations surrounding the intentional creation and breeding of hybrids. It is important to ensure that the process is conducted responsibly and with consideration for the welfare of the fish involved. It is also crucial to avoid hybridization that may negatively impact wild populations or result in the displacement of purebred individuals.

As a responsible aquarium hobbyist, it is recommended to avoid unintentional or uncontrolled crossbreeding of Moonlight Gouramis and prioritize the preservation and appreciation of the purebred species and varieties.

In conclusion, while hybridization can produce visually interesting results, it is essential to understand and consider the potential consequences associated with crossbreeding. Maintaining the genetic integrity and health of the Moonlight Gourami species should be a priority to ensure their long-term conservation and enjoyment in aquarium settings.

Moonlight Gourami

Quarantine Procedures for New Fish

Implementing proper quarantine procedures is essential when introducing new fish, including Moonlight Gouramis, into an aquarium. Quarantine helps prevent the introduction and spread of diseases, parasites, and other harmful organisms, safeguarding the health of existing tank inhabitants. Here are the recommended steps for quarantine:

Isolation Tank Setup

Prepare a separate isolation tank specifically dedicated to the quarantine process. The tank should be appropriately sized, ideally with filtration, a heater, and adequate hiding places to reduce stress for the quarantined fish.

Duration of Quarantine

Quarantine periods may vary, but it is generally recommended to quarantine new fish for a minimum of 2-4 weeks. This duration allows for observation and potential treatment of any underlying health issues that may not be immediately apparent.

Observation and Assessment

During the quarantine period, closely monitor the behavior, appetite, and overall condition of the new Moonlight Gouramis. Look for any signs of disease, such as abnormal swimming, loss of appetite, visible parasites, or physical abnormalities.

Water Parameters and Treatment

Maintain optimal water conditions in the quarantine tank, similar to the parameters of the main display tank. Regularly test and maintain appropriate water temperature, pH levels, ammonia, nitrite, and nitrate levels. If necessary, consult a veterinarian or experienced aquarist for guidance on potential preventive treatments or medications for common fish diseases.

Quarantine Tank Maintenance

Perform regular water changes in the quarantine tank to maintain good water quality. Ensure that all equipment used for the quarantine tank is dedicated solely to that purpose and not shared with the main display tank to prevent cross-contamination.

Observation and Gradual Introduction

Observe the quarantined fish closely throughout the quarantine period. If they remain healthy and show no signs of illness, they can gradually be introduced to the main display tank after the quarantine period ends. This step helps prevent the introduction of potential pathogens or parasites to the established aquarium ecosystem.

By following these quarantine procedures, you can minimize the risk of introducing diseases or parasites to your existing fish population and promote a healthy and thriving aquarium environment for your Moonlight Gouramis and other aquatic inhabitants.

Moonlight Gourami

Native Habitat and Distribution

The Moonlight Gourami, Trichopodus microlepis, is native to Southeast Asia, where it can be found in various freshwater habitats. Let's explore its native habitat and distribution:

Geographical Range

The Moonlight Gourami is endemic to the region of Southeast Asia. Its natural distribution includes countries such as Thailand, Malaysia, Indonesia, and Cambodia.

Freshwater Environments

Within its native range, the Moonlight Gourami inhabits a variety of freshwater environments, including rivers, streams, ponds, and flooded forest areas. It is commonly found in slow-moving or stagnant waters with dense vegetation, such as marshes, swamps, and shallow lakes.

Environmental Conditions

The fish is adapted to thrive in warm tropical conditions. It prefers water temperatures between 75°F to 82°F (24°C to 28°C) and acidic to slightly alkaline pH levels, typically ranging from 6.0 to 7.5.

Vegetation and Cover

Moonlight Gouramis are often associated with areas abundant in aquatic vegetation, including floating plants, submerged vegetation, and marginal vegetation. These plants provide essential cover and shelter, creating a favorable habitat for the fish. The dense vegetation also offers a food source and supports the overall ecological balance of their natural environment.

Interaction with Other Species

Within its native habitat, the Moonlight Gourami coexists with a diverse range of freshwater species. It shares its environment with other fish, including various gourami species, labyrinth fish, barbs, rasboras, catfish, and invertebrates like shrimps and snails.

Conservation and Threats

Due to its wide distribution and adaptable nature, the Moonlight Gourami is currently not considered endangered. However, habitat destruction, water pollution, and overcollection for the aquarium trade can pose threats to its natural populations. It is important to support sustainable practices and responsible sourcing when acquiring Moonlight Gouramis for aquariums.

The Moonlight Gourami's native habitat in Southeast Asia showcases the species' preference for warm, vegetated freshwater environments. Understanding its natural habitat and distribution helps in creating suitable aquarium setups that mimic its original conditions, promoting the well-being and natural behavior of these beautiful fish.

Moonlight Gourami

Behavior and Social Structure

The Moonlight Gourami, Trichopodus microlepis, displays intriguing behavior and exhibits a social structure within its natural habitat and aquarium environments. Let's explore the key aspects of their behavior:

Solitary Nature

Moonlight Gouramis are generally solitary fish, preferring to spend most of their time alone or in small groups. They are known to establish territories within their habitat, especially around dense vegetation or preferred hiding spots.

Nocturnal Activity

These gouramis exhibit a natural tendency for nocturnal activity. They are most active during the evening and night, utilizing their labyrinth organ to breathe atmospheric air from the water's surface. During the day, they often seek shelter or remain hidden among plants or other structures in their environment.

Exploratory Behavior

Moonlight Gouramis are curious fish and engage in exploratory behavior. They enjoy investigating their surroundings, especially when provided with a well-decorated aquarium that includes plants, driftwood, and hiding places. Providing a stimulating environment can help promote their natural behaviors and reduce stress.

Territorial Defense

Male Moonlight Gouramis can exhibit territorial behavior, especially during breeding or when establishing dominance. They may become more aggressive towards conspecifics or other fish encroaching on their territory. Adequate space and visual barriers within the aquarium can help minimize territorial disputes.

Compatibility with Other Fish

When it comes to social interactions, Moonlight Gouramis are generally peaceful and can coexist with a variety of fish species. However, caution should be exercised when selecting tankmates. Avoid housing them with overly aggressive or fin-nipping fish that may cause stress or harm to the gouramis. Peaceful community fish, such as tetras, rasboras, or other gourami species, often make suitable tankmates.

Mating and Breeding Behavior

During the mating season, male Moonlight Gouramis may exhibit courtship behavior, including flaring their fins and displaying vibrant colors to attract females. Mating typically involves the male constructing a bubblenest at the water's surface, where the female deposits eggs. After spawning, it is recommended to remove the female from the breeding tank to prevent aggression from the male.

Understanding the behavior and social structure of Moonlight Gouramis is important for providing an enriching and harmonious environment in an aquarium setting. By promoting their natural behaviors and ensuring compatible tankmates, you can create a peaceful and captivating aquatic habitat.

Moonlight Gourami

Feeding Habits and Diet

The Moonlight Gourami, Trichopodus microlepis, is an omnivorous fish with specific feeding habits and dietary requirements. Understanding their feeding preferences is crucial for providing a well-balanced diet. Let's explore their feeding habits:

Omnivorous Nature

Moonlight Gouramis are classified as omnivores, which means they consume a variety of plant and animal matter. In their natural habitat, they feed on a diverse range of food sources, including insects, small crustaceans, algae, plant matter, and other organic detritus.

Vegetable Matter

Plant matter forms a significant part of the Moonlight Gourami's diet. They consume algae, small aquatic plants, and even fallen plant material from the water's surface. Providing a variety of plant-based foods in the aquarium helps replicate their natural feeding habits.

Live and Frozen Foods

In addition to plant matter, Moonlight Gouramis also benefit from live or frozen foods. They eagerly consume small live foods like brine shrimp, daphnia, and bloodworms. These protein-rich foods provide essential nutrients and help satisfy their natural feeding instincts.

High-Quality Flakes and Pellets

Commercially available high-quality flakes or pellets formulated for tropical fish make an excellent staple diet for Moonlight Gouramis. Look for products specifically designed for gouramis or omnivorous fish. These foods are typically fortified with essential vitamins, minerals, and proteins to support their overall health.

Supplementing with Fresh Vegetables

Adding fresh vegetables to their diet is beneficial for Moonlight Gouramis. Blanched vegetables like spinach, lettuce, zucchini, or cucumber can be offered occasionally. These vegetables provide additional fiber and nutrients and can help diversify their diet.

Feeding Frequency and Portions

It is recommended to feed Moonlight Gouramis small portions multiple times a day rather than a large amount once. This feeding approach mimics their natural feeding behavior and helps prevent overfeeding and potential water quality issues. Monitor their feeding response and adjust the portion size accordingly to avoid excess food waste.

Providing a varied and balanced diet that includes a combination of high-quality flakes, pellets, live or frozen foods, and occasional fresh vegetables will ensure optimal nutrition and promote the overall health and well-being of Moonlight Gouramis in the aquarium setting.

Moonlight Gourami

Reproduction and Breeding Cycle

Moonlight Gouramis, Trichopodus microlepis, have an interesting reproductive behavior and breeding cycle. Let's explore the key aspects of their reproduction:

Breeding Behavior

During the breeding season, male Moonlight Gouramis exhibit territorial and courtship behavior to attract females. The males often develop brighter colors and elongated fins to display their dominance and readiness to mate.

Bubblenest Construction

Once a male has enticed a female to his territory, he will initiate the construction of a bubblenest. The male creates the nest at the water's surface by using bubbles produced from his mouth. The nest serves as a protective structure for the eggs and later the fry.

Spawning and Egg Depositing

After the bubblenest is completed, the female will deposit a batch of eggs into the nest. The male follows closely, fertilizing the eggs as they are released. This process continues until the female has released all her eggs, resulting in a nest containing multiple fertilized eggs.

Male Nest Guardian

After spawning, the male takes on the role of nest guardian. He diligently tends to the bubblenest, protecting it and the developing eggs. The male uses his labyrinth organ to provide oxygen to the eggs by taking in air from the water's surface and passing it over the nest.

Egg Incubation

The incubation period for Moonlight Gourami eggs typically lasts around 24 to 48 hours. During this time, the male maintains the nest, adjusting its position and ensuring proper oxygenation. It is crucial to provide stable water conditions and a calm environment to promote successful egg development.

Hatching and Fry Care

Once the eggs hatch, tiny fry emerge from the bubblenest. Initially, the fry remain attached to the nest through adhesive glands on their bodies. After a few days, they become free-swimming and start exploring their surroundings. At this point, the male may lose interest in guarding the fry.

Fry Feeding and Growth

Once the fry are free-swimming, they require proper nutrition. Infusoria, microorganisms, and commercially available liquid fry food can serve as suitable initial food sources. As the fry grow, their diet can be gradually transitioned to finely crushed flakes or baby brine shrimp.

Understanding the reproductive behavior and breeding cycle of Moonlight Gouramis allows aquarists to create suitable conditions for successful breeding. Providing a well-prepared bubblenest, maintaining stable water conditions, and offering appropriate fry food help ensure the well-being and survival of the next generation of Moonlight Gouramis in the aquarium.

Moonlight Gourami

Water Parameters and Temperature Requirements

Creating the right water conditions is essential for the well-being and optimal health of Moonlight Gouramis, Trichopodus microlepis. Let's explore the key water parameters and temperature requirements for these fish:

Water Temperature

Moonlight Gouramis are tropical fish and thrive in warmer water temperatures. The ideal temperature range for their aquarium is between 75°F to 82°F (24°C to 28°C). Maintaining a stable and appropriate temperature is crucial for their overall health, digestion, and immune system function.

pH Level

These gouramis prefer slightly acidic to slightly alkaline water conditions. The recommended pH range for Moonlight Gouramis is typically between 6.0 to 7.5. It is important to monitor and maintain a stable pH level within this range to support their physiological processes and overall well-being.

Water Hardness

Moonlight Gouramis can tolerate a wide range of water hardness levels. They are adaptable to both soft and moderately hard water conditions. A general guideline is to aim for a water hardness level between 5 to 20 dGH (degrees of general hardness). Ensuring stable water hardness helps prevent fluctuations that could stress the fish.

Water Filtration and Quality

Good water filtration and quality are crucial for maintaining a healthy aquarium environment. Moonlight Gouramis appreciate clean, well-oxygenated water. A reliable filtration system, regular water changes, and the removal of debris and excess waste help ensure optimal water conditions for their well-being.

Aquarium Size and Space

When considering the appropriate aquarium size for Moonlight Gouramis, it is recommended to provide ample swimming space and suitable territory for these fish. A tank size of at least 30 gallons (113 liters) or larger is advisable for a small group of Moonlight Gouramis, allowing them to establish territories and exhibit natural behavior.

Compatibility with Tankmates

When selecting tankmates for Moonlight Gouramis, it is important to consider their compatibility with other fish species. They generally coexist well with peaceful community fish that share similar water parameter requirements. Avoid housing them with aggressive or fin-nipping fish that may cause stress or harm.

By maintaining suitable water parameters and providing a well-maintained aquarium environment, you can ensure the comfort, health, and longevity of Moonlight Gouramis in your care.

Moonlight Gourami

Tankmates: Compatible Species

When selecting tankmates for Moonlight Gouramis, Trichopodus microlepis, it is important to choose species that are compatible in terms of temperament, size, and water parameter requirements. Here are some compatible species to consider:

Tetras

Tetras, such as Neon Tetras (Paracheirodon innesi), Ember Tetras (Hyphessobrycon amandae), or Cardinal Tetras (Paracheirodon axelrodi), make excellent tankmates for Moonlight Gouramis. They are peaceful, schooling fish that add color and activity to the aquarium.

Rasboras

Rasboras, such as Harlequin Rasboras (Trigonostigma heteromorpha) or Chili Rasboras (Boraras brigittae), are peaceful and active fish that coexist well with Moonlight Gouramis. They *prefer similar water parameters and create a lively display in the aquarium.*

Gourami Species

Other gourami species can be suitable tankmates for Moonlight Gouramis, as long as the aquarium is spacious enough to accommodate multiple individuals. Examples include Honey Gouramis (Trichogaster chuna) or Dwarf Gouramis (Trichogaster lalius).

Livebearers

Livebearing fish, such as Platies (Xiphophorus spp.) or Guppies (Poecilia reticulata), can coexist with Moonlight Gouramis. They are colorful, active, and generally peaceful fish that add diversity to the aquarium community.

Corydoras Catfish

Corydoras catfish, such as Bronze Corydoras (Corydoras aeneus) or Peppered Corydoras (Corydoras paleatus), make suitable bottom-dwelling tankmates for Moonlight Gouramis. They help keep the substrate clean and are peaceful companions.

Snails and Shrimp

Aquatic snails, like Nerite Snails (Neritina spp.) or Mystery Snails (Pomacea spp.), can be compatible tankmates for Moonlight Gouramis. Additionally, peaceful shrimp species like Cherry Shrimp (Neocaridina davidi) can also coexist in the aquarium, adding interest and assisting with algae control.

When introducing new tankmates, it is important to monitor their interactions and ensure that all fish are thriving without signs of stress or aggression. Providing ample hiding places, plants, and sufficient swimming space helps promote a harmonious and diverse aquarium community.

Moonlight Gourami

Territoriality and Hierarchy

Moonlight Gouramis, Trichopodus microlepis, exhibit certain territorial and hierarchical behaviors, especially during breeding and establishing dominance. Let's explore their behavior in relation to territoriality and hierarchy:

Male Dominance and Territorial Behavior

Male Moonlight Gouramis can be territorial, especially during the breeding season. They establish and defend their territories, which often include a suitable location for constructing a bubblenest. Males may display aggressive behavior towards other males to assert their dominance and claim their territory.

Aggression and Hierarchy Establishment

When multiple males are present in the same aquarium, aggression may occur as they establish a hierarchy. This can involve displays of flaring fins, chasing, and occasional nipping. The aggression usually subsides once a clear dominance order is established, with the most dominant male gaining control over the territory and breeding rights.

Female Interactions and Courtship

During courtship, male Moonlight Gouramis showcase their territorial behavior to attract females. They display vibrant colors, erect fins, and perform courtship dances to impress the females. Females are generally less aggressive and more accepting of the male's advances, choosing a suitable mate based on their preferences.

Established Hierarchy and Coexistence

Once a hierarchy is established among the male Moonlight Gouramis, they typically coexist peacefully, respecting each other's territories. However, occasional territorial disputes may arise, especially during breeding events or when new fish are introduced. Providing ample hiding spots, plants, and territories within the aquarium can help minimize conflicts.

Territoriality and Tank Size

The size of the aquarium can influence the territorial behavior of Moonlight Gouramis. Providing a larger tank with plenty of swimming space and suitable territories helps reduce territorial disputes and aggression among males. A spacious environment allows each fish to establish and defend its own territory more effectively.

Monitoring the behavior of Moonlight Gouramis and providing a well-designed aquarium setup with appropriate territories and hiding places can help minimize aggression and create a harmonious environment for these beautiful fish.

Moonlight Gourami

Reproduction and Breeding Cycle

Moonlight Gouramis, Trichopodus microlepis, exhibit fascinating reproductive behavior and follow a distinct breeding cycle. Let's explore the key aspects of their reproduction:

Breeding Behavior

During the breeding season, male Moonlight Gouramis display territorial and courtship behavior to attract females. The males often develop brighter colors and elongated fins to demonstrate their dominance and readiness to mate.

Bubblenest Construction

Once a male has enticed a female to his territory, he initiates the construction of a bubblenest. Using bubbles produced from his mouth, the male creates the nest at the water's surface. The nest serves as a protective structure for the eggs and later the fry.

Spawning and Egg Deposition

After the bubblenest is completed, the female deposits a batch of eggs into the nest. The male closely follows, fertilizing the eggs as they are released. This process continues until the female has released all her eggs, resulting in a nest containing multiple fertilized eggs.

Male Nest Guardian

After spawning, the male assumes the role of nest guardian. He diligently tends to the bubblenest, protecting it and the developing eggs. The male uses his labyrinth organ to provide oxygen to the eggs by taking in air from the water's surface and passing it over the nest.

Egg Incubation

The incubation period for Moonlight Gourami eggs typically lasts around 24 to 48 hours. During this time, the male maintains the nest, adjusting its position and ensuring proper oxygenation. It is crucial to provide stable water conditions and a calm environment to promote successful egg development.

Hatching and Fry Care

Once the eggs hatch, tiny fry emerge from the bubblenest. Initially, the fry remain attached to the nest through adhesive glands on their bodies. After a few days, they become free-swimming and start exploring their surroundings. At this point, the male may lose interest in guarding the fry.

Fry Feeding and Growth

Once the fry are free-swimming, they require appropriate nutrition. Infusoria, microorganisms, and commercially available liquid fry food can serve as suitable initial food sources. As the fry grow, their diet can be gradually transitioned to finely crushed flakes or baby brine shrimp.

Understanding the reproductive behavior and breeding cycle of Moonlight Gouramis enables aquarists to create suitable conditions for successful breeding. Providing a well-prepared bubblenest, maintaining stable water conditions, and offering appropriate fry food help ensure the well-being and survival of the next generation of Moonlight Gouramis in the aquarium.

Moonlight Gourami

Common Diseases and Health Issues

Moonlight Gouramis, *Trichopodus microlepis*, are generally hardy fish when provided with proper care and optimal water conditions. However, they can be susceptible to certain diseases and health issues. Here are some common ailments to be aware of:

1. Ich (White Spot Disease)

Ich is a parasitic disease characterized by the presence of white spots on the fish's body, fins, and gills. It is caused by the protozoan parasite *Ichthyophthirius multifiliis*. Ich is highly contagious and can be triggered by stress or fluctuations in water parameters. Prompt treatment with appropriate medication and improving water quality are essential for curing this disease.

2. Fin Rot

Fin Rot is a bacterial infection that affects the fins and can lead to fin deterioration. Poor water quality, stress, and injuries are common causes of Fin Rot. Symptoms include frayed or eroding fins, discoloration, and inflammation. Treating the fish with antibacterial medications and addressing the underlying causes are important for healing and preventing further fin damage.

3. Fungal Infections

Fungal infections can occur on wounds or damaged areas of the fish, often as a secondary infection. Symptoms include cotton-like growths, fuzzy patches, or white/greyish spots on the body or fins. Treating the affected areas with antifungal medications and ensuring good water quality aids in resolving fungal infections.

4. Swim Bladder Disorder

Swim bladder disorder affects the fish's ability to control its buoyancy, causing them to float or sink uncontrollably. It can be caused by various factors, including overfeeding, poor diet, or bacterial infections. Providing a balanced diet, avoiding overfeeding, and maintaining good water quality can help prevent swim bladder disorders.

5. Stress-Related Issues

Moonlight Gouramis can be susceptible to stress-related issues, such as poor appetite, weakened immune system, and increased susceptibility to diseases. Stressors include inappropriate water conditions, aggressive tankmates, overcrowding, or sudden changes in the environment. Maintaining stable water parameters, providing suitable tankmates, and minimizing stressors help promote the overall health and well-being of these fish.

Regular observation of Moonlight Gouramis, maintaining optimal water conditions, and promptly addressing any signs of illness are essential for keeping them healthy. Consulting with a knowledgeable aquarist or veterinarian can provide further guidance in diagnosing and treating specific diseases or health issues.

Moonlight Gourami

Recognizing and Treating Common Diseases

Moonlight Gouramis, Trichopodus microlepis, can be affected by various diseases. Recognizing the symptoms and promptly treating them is crucial for the well-being of these fish. Here are some common diseases and their treatments:

1. Ich (White Spot Disease)

Ich is characterized by the presence of white spots on the fish's body, fins, and gills. Treatments include raising the tank temperature to around 86°F (30°C) to speed up the parasite life cycle, using medications containing malachite green or copper sulfate, and improving water quality. Follow the instructions provided with the medication and continue treatment until all signs of the disease have disappeared.

2. Fin Rot

Symptoms of Fin Rot include frayed or eroding fins, discoloration, and inflammation. To treat Fin Rot, start by improving water quality through regular water changes. Additionally, use antibacterial medications specifically formulated for fin issues. Ensure that the medication is safe for use with Gouramis and follow the instructions for dosage and duration of treatment.

3. Fungal Infections

If you notice cotton-like growths, fuzzy patches, or white/greyish spots on the body or fins of your Moonlight Gourami, it may indicate a fungal infection. Treat the affected areas with antifungal medications, such as those containing malachite green or methylene blue. Ensure that the medication is suitable for Gouramis and follow the recommended dosage and treatment duration.

4. Swim Bladder Disorder

Swim bladder disorders can cause buoyancy issues in Moonlight Gouramis. If your fish is having difficulty swimming or is floating or sinking uncontrollably, it may be suffering from this disorder. Treatment options include feeding a high-fiber diet to aid digestion, fasting the fish for a few days, and providing a stress-free environment. If the condition persists, consult a veterinarian for further guidance.

5. Stress-Related Issues

Stress-related issues can weaken the immune system of Moonlight Gouramis, making them more susceptible to diseases. Identify and address the stressors in the aquarium, such as poor water quality, aggressive tankmates, or sudden environmental changes. Maintaining stable water parameters, providing hiding places, and reducing stressors can help improve the fish's overall health.

It is important to remember that accurate diagnosis is crucial for effective treatment. If you are uncertain about the specific disease or need further guidance, consult with an experienced aquarist or a veterinarian who specializes in fish health. They can provide tailored advice and recommend appropriate medications or treatments for your Moonlight Gouramis.

Moonlight Gourami

Prevention and Treatment of Diseases

Preventing diseases and promptly treating them is vital for maintaining the health of Moonlight Gouramis, Trichopodus microlepis. Here are some preventive measures and treatment strategies:

1. Quarantine New Fish

Quarantine newly acquired fish before introducing them to your main aquarium. This helps prevent the spread of potential diseases to your existing fish population. Observe the quarantined fish for any signs of illness and treat them if necessary before introducing them to the main tank.

2. Maintain Optimal Water Conditions

Provide clean and stable water conditions for your Moonlight Gouramis. Regularly monitor and maintain appropriate temperature, pH levels, and ammonia/nitrite/nitrate levels. Perform regular water changes to remove accumulated toxins and maintain water quality.

3. Avoid Overcrowding

Avoid overcrowding your aquarium as it can lead to increased stress and higher chances of disease outbreaks. Provide sufficient swimming space and territory for each fish. Research the appropriate tank size and recommended number of Moonlight Gouramis to ensure their well-being.

4. Balanced Diet and Feeding Practices

Provide a balanced diet that meets the nutritional needs of Moonlight Gouramis. Feed them a variety of high-quality foods, including pellets, flakes, and frozen/live foods. Avoid overfeeding, as it can lead to digestive issues and poor water quality. Feed them in small portions multiple times a day.

5. Quarantine and Treat Diseased Fish

If you observe any signs of disease in your Moonlight Gouramis, promptly isolate the affected fish in a separate quarantine tank. Treat the fish according to the specific disease using appropriate medications as recommended by a veterinarian or experienced aquarist. Follow the treatment instructions carefully and complete the full course of treatment.

6. Stress Reduction

Minimize stress factors in the aquarium, as stress weakens the fish's immune system and makes them more susceptible to diseases. Provide hiding places, maintain a peaceful tank environment, avoid sudden changes in water conditions, and ensure compatibility among tankmates.

By following these preventive measures and promptly treating any diseases that arise, you can help ensure the health and well-being of your Moonlight Gouramis. Regular monitoring, responsible fishkeeping practices, and seeking professional advice when needed are essential for maintaining a thriving and disease-free aquarium.

Moonlight Gourami

Life Cycle and Growth Stages

Moonlight Gouramis, Trichopodus microlepis, go through various stages of development as they grow and mature. Let's explore the different life cycle stages of these fish:

Egg Stage

The life cycle begins with the egg stage. After successful fertilization, the female Moonlight Gourami deposits the eggs into the male's bubblenest. The eggs are adhesive and stick to the nest, where they are protected and cared for by the male. The incubation period typically lasts around 24 to 48 hours.

Fry Stage

Once the eggs hatch, the fry emerge from the bubblenest. Initially, they remain attached to the nest through adhesive glands on their bodies. Over the next few days, the fry become free-swimming and start exploring their environment.

At this stage, they are very small and delicate, requiring special care and suitable food sources.

Juvenile Stage

As the fry grow, they enter the juvenile stage. During this stage, the Moonlight Gouramis develop their characteristic body shape and coloration. They continue to grow in size and gradually develop the distinctive fins and other features of adult gouramis. Juveniles are still relatively small and require proper nutrition and optimal water conditions for healthy growth.

Adult Stage

The final stage of the life cycle is the adult stage. At this point, Moonlight Gouramis have reached their full size and have developed their mature coloration and patterns. Adult gouramis are sexually mature and capable of reproducing. They exhibit the characteristic behaviors and social dynamics associated with their species.

The life cycle and growth stages of Moonlight Gouramis demonstrate the natural progression of these fish from eggs to adults. Providing suitable conditions, proper nutrition, and attentive care *throughout each stage are essential for their healthy development and overall well-being.*

Moonlight Gourami

Selecting Healthy Fish: Buying and Quarantine Process

When purchasing Moonlight Gouramis, it is important to select healthy specimens to ensure their well-being in your aquarium. Here are some guidelines for buying and quarantining these fish:

1. Choosing a Reputable Retailer

Buy Moonlight Gouramis from reputable fish stores or breeders known for their quality and healthy stock. Research and seek recommendations from experienced aquarists to find reliable sources. Reputable retailers prioritize the health and care of their fish, increasing the chances of obtaining healthy specimens.

2. Visual Inspection

Observe the fish closely before making a purchase. Look for the following signs of a healthy Moonlight Gourami:

- Bright and vibrant coloration
- Clear and undamaged fins
- No visible signs of disease (e.g., white spots, torn fins, abnormal growths)
- Active and alert behavior
- Normal swimming and breathing

Avoid purchasing fish that show signs of stress, lethargy, or obvious health issues.

3. Quarantine Process

After purchasing Moonlight Gouramis, it is essential to quarantine them before introducing them to your main aquarium. Quarantine serves two main purposes:

1. Preventing the introduction of diseases or parasites to your existing fish population.
2. Allowing you to closely monitor and treat any potential health issues in the new fish without affecting other tank inhabitants.

Set up a separate quarantine tank with appropriate filtration, temperature, and water conditions. Observe the new fish for signs of disease or stress during the quarantine period, which typically lasts a few weeks. If any health issues arise, treat the fish accordingly using appropriate medications and follow the recommended treatment duration.

4. Monitoring and Acclimation

Regularly monitor the quarantined fish for any signs of illness or abnormal behavior. Pay attention to their appetite, swimming patterns, and overall condition. Once the quarantine period is complete and the fish are deemed healthy, gradually acclimate them to the main aquarium by slowly adjusting the water parameters and temperature. This helps minimize stress and facilitates a smooth transition for the fish.

By following these guidelines and taking the necessary precautions, you can increase the chances of selecting healthy Moonlight Gouramis and minimize the risk of introducing diseases to your aquarium. Quarantining new fish is a crucial step in maintaining the overall health and well-being of your aquatic community.

Moonlight Gourami

Hybridization: Crossbreeding and Its Consequences

Moonlight Gouramis, Trichopodus microlepis, have been crossbred with other gourami species, leading to the creation of hybrid offspring. Here's an overview of hybridization and its consequences:

1. Crossbreeding Process

Crossbreeding involves mating Moonlight Gouramis with other gourami species, either intentionally or unintentionally. This can occur in home aquariums, fish farms, or during transportation or storage with different gourami species. Hybridization may also occur naturally in regions where different gourami species coexist in the wild.

2. Hybrid Appearance

Hybrid Moonlight Gouramis may exhibit a combination of physical traits from both parent species. This can result in variations in coloration, body shape, fin structure, and other characteristics. The specific appearance of hybrid offspring depends on the genetic contributions from each parent species.

3. Hybrid Vigor

Hybridization can sometimes result in offspring that display enhanced vigor and growth compared to the parent species. This phenomenon, known as hybrid vigor or heterosis, may lead to improved adaptability, resistance to diseases, or other beneficial traits. However, not all hybrid offspring exhibit increased vigor, and the outcomes can be unpredictable.

4. Genetic Integrity

Hybridization can pose risks to the genetic integrity of the parent species. When hybridization occurs frequently, it can lead to the dilution of genetic traits specific to the original Moonlight Gourami species. This can impact the overall genetic diversity and purity of the parent species population.

5. Conservation Concerns

Hybridization can also have implications for conservation efforts. If hybrid offspring are introduced into natural habitats or released into the wild, they can potentially hybridize with native populations, leading to genetic introgression and potential loss of genetic uniqueness. This is of particular concern when dealing with endangered or threatened gourami species.

It is important for aquarists and breeders to be mindful of the consequences of hybridization and its potential impact on the genetic integrity of Moonlight Gouramis and other gourami species. Responsible breeding practices, species-specific housing, and avoiding unintentional crossbreeding are essential for preserving the genetic diversity and integrity of these fish species.

Moonlight Gourami

Preparing for Breeding

If you're interested in breeding Moonlight Gouramis, Trichopodus microlepis, proper preparation is essential to increase the chances of successful reproduction. Here are some key steps to follow when preparing these fish for breeding:

1. Tank Setup

Set up a separate breeding tank that provides suitable conditions for the breeding pair. The tank should have a capacity of at least 20 gallons and be equipped with appropriate filtration and heating systems. Create hiding places using plants, rocks, or other aquarium decorations to mimic the natural environment of Moonlight Gouramis.

2. Conditioning the Breeding Pair

Condition the breeding pair by providing them with a nutritious and varied diet. Offer live or frozen foods such as brine shrimp, bloodworms, and daphnia to enhance their overall health and stimulate reproductive behaviors. Conditioning the fish with high-quality foods for a few weeks before breeding can improve their chances of successful reproduction.

3. Adjusting Water Parameters

To induce breeding, make gradual adjustments to the water parameters in the breeding tank. Increase the temperature slightly to around 80-82°F (26-28°C) and maintain a slightly acidic to neutral pH level between 6.5 and 7.0. Conduct regular water tests and ensure proper filtration and water circulation to maintain stable and optimal conditions.

4. Introducing the Breeding Pair

Once the fish are adequately conditioned and the tank conditions are suitable, introduce the male and female Moonlight Gouramis into the breeding tank. Monitor their behavior closely for signs of courtship and breeding activity. It is advisable to have one male and multiple females to reduce the chances of aggression and increase the breeding success rate.

5. Observe Breeding Behavior

During the breeding process, the male will construct a bubblenest at the water surface. The male will entice the female beneath the nest to deposit her eggs, after which he fertilizes them. The male will guard the nest and eggs, while the female should be removed from the tank to prevent her from eating the eggs.

6. Post-Breeding Care

After successful breeding, it is important to provide proper care for the eggs and fry. Maintain stable water conditions, ensure the bubblenest remains intact, and avoid any disturbances to the breeding tank. Once the fry hatch and become free-swimming, they can be fed with infusoria or commercially available fry foods suitable for their tiny size.

Proper preparation and attentive care are essential when breeding Moonlight Gouramis. It is important to note that breeding fish can be challenging and may require experience and patience. Monitoring water parameters, maintaining optimal conditions, and providing appropriate nutrition will enhance the chances of a successful breeding endeavor.

Moonlight Gourami

Spawning Process and Parental Care

Moonlight Gouramis, Trichopodus microlepis, exhibit interesting behaviors during the spawning process and display remarkable parental care. Let's explore the spawning process and the parental care exhibited by these fish:

Spawning Process

The spawning process of Moonlight Gouramis involves several distinct steps:

1. Courtship: The male initiates courtship by displaying vibrant colors and elaborate fin movements to attract the female's attention.
2. Bubble nest Construction: The male builds a bubble nest at the water surface using air bubbles and saliva. The nest serves as a safe haven for the eggs.
3. Egg Deposition: The female is enticed by the male beneath the bubble nest, where she releases her eggs. The male fertilizes the eggs immediately.
4. Guarding the Nest: The male guards the nest, diligently tending to the eggs and maintaining the integrity of the bubble nest.

5. Egg Hatching: The eggs typically hatch within 24 to 48 hours, and the fry emerge from the nest.

Parental Care

Moonlight Gouramis are known for their remarkable parental care, primarily provided by the male. Here's an overview of their parental behaviors:

- Nest Maintenance: The male gourami actively tends to the bubble nest, repairing any damage and reinforcing it with additional bubbles.
- Protection: The male fiercely guards the nest and the hatched fry. He drives away potential threats or predators, ensuring the safety of the offspring.
- Fry Retrieval: If any fry fall out of the nest, the male carefully picks them up in his mouth and spits them back into the nest.
- Nest Repair: As the fry grow and become more active, the male may reinforce the nest by adding more bubbles to prevent the fry from escaping.
- Feeding Assistance: Initially, the fry derive nourishment from their yolk sacs. Once they become free-swimming, the male assists by herding the fry under the nest and providing them with small, newly hatched live foods.

The parental care exhibited by Moonlight Gouramis contributes to the survival and *development of the offspring. It demonstrates the dedication and protective nature of these fish during the crucial stages of reproduction and early fry rearing.*

Moonlight Gourami

Raising Fish Fry: *Care* and Feeding

Raising Moonlight Gourami fry requires special attention and appropriate feeding to ensure their healthy growth and development. Here are some key considerations for caring and feeding the fry:

1. Suitable Tank Setup

Transfer the fry to a separate rearing tank once they become free-swimming. The rearing tank should have a gentle water flow, adequate filtration, and aeration to maintain good water quality. Provide hiding places such as plants or fine mesh nets to protect the fry from larger tankmates and potential predators.

2. Feeding the Fry

Moonlight Gourami fry initially feed on their yolk sacs, but as they absorb the yolk and become free-swimming, it is important to start providing them with appropriate food. Here are some options for feeding the fry:

- Infusoria: Feed the fry infusoria, which are microscopic organisms that can be cultured at home or purchased from pet stores. Infusoria provide a suitable size of food for the tiny fry.
- Commercial Fry Foods: Once the fry grow slightly larger, you can introduce commercially available liquid or powdered fry foods. These foods are specifically formulated to meet the nutritional needs of young fish.
- Baby Brine Shrimp: As the fry continue to grow, you can gradually introduce newly hatched baby brine shrimp. These small live organisms are highly nutritious and can help promote healthy growth.

3. Feeding Frequency

Initially, feed the fry small amounts of food multiple times throughout the day. As they grow and their digestive systems develop, gradually reduce the feeding frequency to 2-3 times a day. Observe the fry closely during feeding to ensure they consume the food and adjust the amount accordingly to avoid overfeeding.

4. Water Quality and Maintenance

Maintaining excellent water quality is crucial for the health and well-being of the fry. Regularly monitor water parameters such as temperature, pH, and ammonia levels. Perform partial water changes to keep the water clean and stable. Avoid sudden fluctuations in water parameters, as they can be stressful for the fry.

5. Growth and Development

As the fry grow, you will notice their development and increased activity. Provide a suitable environment with appropriate hiding places and adequate space for them to swim and explore. Regularly monitor their growth and make sure to remove any sick or weak fry to prevent the spread of diseases.

Remember, raising fry requires patience and careful attention to their needs. Providing a nutritious diet, maintaining optimal water conditions, and ensuring a safe environment will help the Moonlight Gourami fry thrive and grow into healthy adults.

Moonlight Gourami

Tank Troubleshooting: Algae Control and Water Quality Issues

Keeping a well-maintained aquarium is crucial for the health and well-being of Moonlight Gouramis. Here are some common tank troubleshooting tips to control algae growth and maintain optimal water quality:

1. Algae Control

Algae growth is a common issue in aquariums. While some algae is normal and even beneficial, excessive growth can be unsightly and potentially harmful to the fish. Here are some strategies for controlling algae:

- Lighting: Adjust the duration and intensity of the aquarium lighting. Algae thrives in excessive light, so reducing the lighting period or using a timer to provide consistent lighting can help control algae growth.
- Nutrient Management: Algae feed on nutrients present in the water, such as nitrates and phosphates. Regular water

changes and proper filtration can help reduce the nutrient levels and inhibit algae growth.
- *Algae Eaters*: Introduce compatible algae-eating species, such as Siamese algae eaters, Otocinclus catfish, or Amano shrimp, to help naturally control algae by consuming it.
- *Manual Removal*: Perform regular maintenance tasks, including manually removing visible algae from the aquarium glass, decorations, and plants. Use a clean algae scraper or brush to gently scrub off the algae.

2. Water Quality Issues

Maintaining good water quality is essential for the health of Moonlight Gouramis. Here are some common water quality issues and how to address them:

- *Ammonia and Nitrite Spikes*: Monitor ammonia and nitrite levels regularly, as high levels can be toxic to fish. Perform regular water changes, avoid overfeeding, and ensure proper biological filtration to prevent ammonia and nitrite spikes.
- *Nitrate Accumulation*: Nitrate is a byproduct of the nitrogen cycle and can accumulate in the aquarium over time. Regular water changes and the use of live plants can help reduce nitrate levels. Additionally, ensure proper filtration and avoid overstocking the tank.

- pH Imbalance: Maintain a stable pH level within the appropriate range for Moonlight Gouramis (pH 6.5 to 7.5). Avoid drastic fluctuations in pH, as it can stress the fish. Use pH stabilizers if necessary, but make changes gradually to avoid shocking the fish.
- Temperature Fluctuations: Sudden temperature changes can be stressful for fish. Use a reliable aquarium heater and thermometer to maintain a consistent temperature within the recommended range for Moonlight Gouramis (75-82°F or 24-28°C).

Regular monitoring of water parameters, proper filtration, regular maintenance, and suitable tank management techniques can help control algae growth and maintain optimal water quality for your Moonlight Gouramis, promoting a healthy and thriving aquarium environment.

Moonlight Gourami

Aquatic Plants: Suitable Choices

Including live aquatic plants in your Moonlight Gourami's aquarium not only enhances its visual appeal but also provides numerous benefits such as oxygenation, natural hiding places, and nutrient absorption. Here are some suitable choices for aquatic plants:

1. Java Fern (*Microsorum pteropus*)

The Java Fern is a popular choice among aquarium enthusiasts. It has sturdy, leathery leaves that are resistant to nibbling by fish. Java Fern can be attached to driftwood or rocks, and it thrives in low to moderate lighting conditions.

2. Amazon Sword (*Echinodorus sp.*)

The Amazon Sword is a large and robust plant that serves as an excellent centerpiece. It has broad, lush leaves that provide shade and cover for the fish. This plant requires moderate lighting and nutrient-rich substrate to thrive.

3. Anubias (Anubias sp.)

Anubias plants have dark, thick leaves that are resistant to herbivorous fish. They are best attached to driftwood or rocks and prefer low to moderate lighting conditions. Anubias plants are hardy and require minimal maintenance.

4. Water Sprite (Ceratopteris thalictroides)

Water Sprite is a versatile floating plant that can also be rooted. It has delicate, finely divided leaves that create a lush appearance. This plant provides cover and shade for the fish and grows well in various lighting conditions.

5. Vallisneria (Vallisneria sp.)

Vallisneria, also known as Vallis or Eelgrass, is a popular choice for larger aquariums. It features long, ribbon-like leaves that create a natural and graceful look. Vallisneria prefers moderate to high lighting and nutrient-rich substrate.

6. Java Moss (Taxiphyllum barbieri)

Java Moss is a versatile and hardy plant that can be attached to various surfaces, including rocks, driftwood, or substrate. It forms dense, lush carpets or provides hiding spots for the fish. Java Moss thrives in low to moderate lighting conditions.

When selecting aquatic plants for your Moonlight Gourami's tank, consider the lighting and nutrient requirements of the plants, as well as their compatibility with your aquarium setup. A well-planted tank not only creates a natural and aesthetically pleasing environment but also contributes to the overall well-being of your fish.

Moonlight Gourami

Caring for Fry: Raising the Next Generation

Raising Moonlight Gourami fry can be a rewarding and exciting experience. Proper care and attention are essential to ensure the healthy growth and development of the next generation. Here are some key considerations for caring for the fry:

1. Separation and Rearing Tank

Once the fry become free-swimming, it is advisable to separate them from the adult fish and transfer them to a dedicated rearing tank. This allows you to provide specific care and closely monitor their progress without the risk of predation or competition for food.

2. Water Quality

Maintaining excellent water quality is crucial for the fry's health. Regularly monitor and maintain proper water parameters, including temperature, pH, ammonia, nitrite, and nitrate levels. Perform regular water changes and ensure efficient filtration to keep the water clean and stable.

3. Feeding

Moonlight Gourami fry have small mouths and require appropriately sized food. Here are some feeding considerations:

- Infusoria: Initially, feed the fry infusoria, which are microscopic organisms that can be cultured at home or purchased from pet stores. They provide a suitable size of food for the tiny fry.
- Commercial Fry Foods: As the fry grow, you can introduce commercially available liquid or powdered fry foods. These specialized foods are formulated to meet the nutritional needs of young fish.
- Baby Brine Shrimp: Once the fry are slightly larger, you can gradually introduce newly hatched baby brine shrimp, which are highly nutritious and aid in their growth.

Ensure that the fry are actively feeding and adjust the feeding frequency and portion sizes accordingly to avoid overfeeding and maintain good water quality.

4. Hiding Places

Provide ample hiding places for the fry to help them feel secure. Live plants, fine mesh nets, or commercial fry-rearing devices can serve as hiding spots, protecting them from potential stressors and larger tankmates.

5. Growth Monitoring

Regularly monitor the fry's growth and overall health. Remove any weak or sick individuals promptly to prevent the spread of diseases and maintain optimal conditions for the remaining fry.

6. Gradual Introduction to Adult Tank

Once the fry have grown to a suitable size and can fend for themselves, you can consider gradually introducing them to the adult tank. Monitor their behavior and ensure that they can integrate without being bullied or stressed by larger fish.

Caring for Moonlight Gourami fry requires attention to detail and a commitment to their well-being. With proper care, you can witness their growth and development, contributing to the success of the next generation of these beautiful fish.

Moonlight Gourami

Aquascaping for Tanks

Aquascaping refers to the art of creating visually appealing and natural-looking underwater landscapes in aquariums. When designing an aquascape for a tank housing Moonlight Gouramis, there are several factors to consider. Here are some key considerations for aquascaping:

1. Natural Environment

Aquascaping should aim to mimic the natural environment of Moonlight Gouramis. Research their native habitat, which typically includes lush vegetation, driftwood, and rocks. Use these elements to create a natural and visually appealing landscape in the tank.

2. Plant Selection

Choose aquatic plants that are compatible with Moonlight Gouramis and their tank requirements. Select a variety of plant species to create different levels and textures in the aquascape. Consider using foreground, midground, and background plants to create depth and visual interest.

3. Hardscape Elements

Incorporate hardscape elements such as driftwood, rocks, or stone into the aquascape. These provide hiding spots and natural focal points. Arrange the hardscape to create caves, crevices, and interesting structures that mimic natural formations.

4. Balance and Proportion

Achieve a sense of balance and proportion in the aquascape by considering the size and growth patterns of the chosen plants and hardscape elements. Avoid overcrowding the tank, as it can lead to poor water circulation and hinder the fish's movement.

5. Lighting and Placement

Consider the lighting requirements of the selected plants and position them accordingly in the tank. Some plants prefer more intense lighting, while others thrive in lower light conditions. Adjust the lighting and placement to create a visually appealing and suitable environment for both the fish and the plants.

6. Open Swimming Space

Provide open swimming spaces for Moonlight Gouramis to move freely. Avoid cluttering the tank with too many decorations or plants, leaving ample space for the fish to explore and exhibit their natural behaviors.

7. Maintenance and Pruning

Regularly maintain the aquascape by trimming and pruning plants to prevent overgrowth. Remove any dead or decaying plant material promptly to maintain water quality. Perform routine maintenance tasks such as water changes and cleaning to keep the tank in optimal condition.

A well-planned and carefully executed aquascape can create a beautiful and natural environment for Moonlight Gouramis, enhancing their well-being and providing an aesthetically pleasing display for aquarium enthusiasts to enjoy.

Moonlight Gourami

Creating Community Tanks

Moonlight Gouramis can be a wonderful addition to a community tank, provided that appropriate tankmates are chosen. When creating a community tank with Moonlight Gouramis, it's important to consider their compatibility with other fish species. Here are some key considerations:

1. Peaceful and Non-Aggressive Species

Moonlight Gouramis are generally peaceful fish, so it's best to select tankmates that share a similar temperament. Avoid aggressive or fin-nipping species that may harass or stress the gouramis.

2. Fish Size

Consider the size of potential tankmates relative to Moonlight Gouramis. Avoid pairing them with significantly smaller fish that may be seen as prey or with larger fish that may intimidate or outcompete them for food and space.

3. Swimming Level

Select fish that occupy different levels of the water column to utilize the tank space efficiently. Choose species that primarily swim in the mid or lower levels to complement the Moonlight Gouramis, which tend to occupy the upper and middle regions.

4. Compatibility with Water Parameters

Ensure that the selected tankmates have similar water parameter requirements as Moonlight Gouramis. This includes factors such as temperature, pH, and water hardness. Compatibility in water conditions promotes overall health and well-being for all fish in the tank.

5. Bottom-Dwelling Species

Incorporate bottom-dwelling species such as Corydoras catfish or small loaches to add diversity and activity to the tank. These species help to clean up excess food and debris from the substrate, contributing to the overall cleanliness of the aquarium.

6. Schooling Fish

Add schooling fish like tetras or rasboras to create a vibrant and active community. These species tend to thrive when kept in groups, providing an appealing visual display and a natural behavior pattern.

7. Observation and Monitoring

Regularly observe and monitor the tank inhabitants for signs of aggression, stress, or compatibility issues. If any conflicts arise, be prepared to make necessary adjustments by rearranging the tank or rehoming certain fish to maintain a harmonious community.

Remember to research the specific requirements and behaviors of potential tankmates before introducing them to ensure a peaceful and thriving community tank. Proper selection and careful monitoring will result in a visually stunning and harmonious aquarium environment.

Moonlight Gourami

In the Wild: Observations and Studies

Studying Moonlight Gouramis in their natural habitat provides valuable insights into their behavior, ecology, and conservation. Here are some observations and studies conducted on Moonlight Gouramis in the wild:

1. Habitat and Distribution

Moonlight Gouramis are native to freshwater habitats in Southeast Asia, including Thailand, Cambodia, Vietnam, and Malaysia. Researchers have conducted surveys and field studies to identify their specific distribution range and the types of environments they inhabit.

2. Behavior and Social Structure

Observations in the wild have revealed various aspects of Moonlight Gourami behavior. Studies have focused on their feeding habits, mating rituals, territoriality, and social interactions within their natural habitat. These studies help understand their natural behavior and provide insights into their needs in captivity.

3. Reproduction and Breeding

Researchers have observed the reproductive behavior and breeding strategies of Moonlight Gouramis in their natural environment. They have documented the spawning process, parental care, and the role of environmental factors in triggering reproduction. These studies contribute to our understanding of their reproductive biology and aid in successful breeding in captivity.

4. *Ecology and Interactions*

Studies have investigated the ecological role of Moonlight Gouramis in their native ecosystems. They are known to feed on insects, small crustaceans, and plant matter. Researchers have explored their impact on prey populations, as well as their interactions with other fish species, predators, and prey.

5. Threats and *Conservation*

Researchers have assessed the threats facing Moonlight Gouramis in the wild, including habitat loss, water pollution, and overfishing. These studies contribute to conservation efforts by providing data on population trends, identifying critical habitats, and supporting initiatives for their protection and sustainable management.

6. Habitat Preservation and Restoration

Studies on the habitat preferences of Moonlight Gouramis help guide conservation initiatives. By understanding their habitat requirements, researchers can contribute to habitat preservation and restoration efforts, ensuring the availability of suitable environments for these fish in the wild.

The knowledge gained from observing Moonlight Gouramis in the wild is vital for their conservation and management. These studies deepen our understanding of their natural behavior, ecological significance, and the challenges they face, ultimately supporting efforts to protect and preserve their populations in their native habitats.

Moonlight Gourami

Conclusion

Moonlight Gouramis are fascinating fish known for their stunning appearance, peaceful nature, and interesting behaviors. With their shimmering scales and elegant fins, they make a captivating addition to any aquarium. From their early history and physical characteristics to their breeding habits and tank requirements, we have explored various aspects of these remarkable fish.

Understanding the genetics, color varieties, and potential consequences of hybridization helps aquarists make informed decisions about breeding programs and maintaining the integrity of Moonlight Gourami populations. Furthermore, being aware of their native habitat, behavior, and social structure allows us to create suitable environments and select compatible tankmates for these fish.

Proper care, including providing a balanced diet, optimal water parameters, and a harmonious tank community, promotes the health and well-being of Moonlight Gouramis.

Recognizing common diseases, their symptoms, and implementing effective prevention and treatment measures are essential for ensuring their longevity in captivity.

Additionally, understanding the life cycle, growth stages, and breeding process of Moonlight Gouramis enables enthusiasts to successfully raise their fry and contribute to the conservation of this species. By implementing proper aquascaping techniques and creating community tanks that mimic their natural environment, we can provide them with a safe and enriching habitat.

In conclusion, Moonlight Gouramis are captivating fish with their unique beauty and peaceful demeanor. With proper care, attention to their specific needs, and a commitment to their conservation, these fish can thrive in aquariums, bringing joy and tranquility to their keepers. We wish all enthusiasts the best in their breeding endeavors and the successful growth of their Moonlight Gourami populations.

Printed in the USA
CPSIA information can be obtained
at www.ICGtesting.com
CBHW051013041224
18424CB00025B/196